Forgiveness

Julie Murray

Abdo
CHARACTER EDUCATION
Kids

abdopublishing.com

Published by Abdo Kids, a division of ABDO, PO Box 398166, Minneapolis, Minnesota 55439.
Copyright © 2018 by Abdo Consulting Group, Inc. International copyrights reserved in all countries.
No part of this book may be reproduced in any form without written permission from the publisher.

Printed in the United States of America, North Mankato, Minnesota.

052017

092017

THIS BOOK CONTAINS
RECYCLED MATERIALS

Photo Credits: iStock, Shutterstock

Production Contributors: Teddy Borth, Jennie Forsberg, Grace Hansen

Design Contributors: Christina Doffing, Candice Keimig, Dorothy Toth

Publisher's Cataloging in Publication Data

Names: Murray, Julie, 1969-, author.

Title: Forgiveness / by Julie Murray.

Description: Minneapolis, Minnesota : Abdo Kids, 2018 | Series: Character
    education | Includes bibliographical references and index.

Identifiers: LCCN 2016962324 | ISBN 9781532100093 (lib. bdg.) |
    ISBN 9781532100789 (ebook) | ISBN 9781532101335 (Read-to-me ebook)

Subjects: LCSH: Forgiveness--Juvenile literature. | Forgiveness in children--Juvenile literature. | Children--
    Conduct of life--Juvenile literature. | Social skills in children--Juvenile literature.

Classification: DDC 179/.9--dc23

LC record available at http://lccn.loc.gov/2016962324

Table of Contents

Forgiveness

Forgiveness is all around.

Do you see it?

Al took Amy's bag.

She gets mad!

Al says, "I'm sorry."

She forgives him.

9

Sue pushed Jim. She says,
"I'm sorry."

Jim forgives her. They play in the **pond**.

Gus is sad. He was **left behind**.

Kyle says, "I'm sorry."

Everyone feels better.

This is forgiveness.

It is hard to do.

Did you forgive today?

More Ways to Forgive

give a high five

give a hug

listen and accept apologies

shake hands

Glossary

left behind
purposefully forgotten.

pond
a body of water smaller than
a lake.

Index

abdokids.com

Use this code to log on to abdokids.com and access crafts, games, videos, and more!

Abdo Kids Code:
CFK0093